Sepia Sentiments

Summer Sayed

BookLeaf Publishing

India | USA | UK

Made with ❤ on the BookLeaf Publishing Platform
www.bookleafpub.in
www.bookleafpub.com

Dedication

"For my parents,
loved and cherished,
forever lost
but never forgotten."

Preface

Sepia Sentiments is a collection of 26 poems that traverse landscapes both internal and external, capturing intense and subtle emotions, stark realities, and the ceaseless passage of time.

Like the sepia tones of an old photograph, these poems are tinged with nostalgia, deep reflection, and the enigma of untold stories.

They journey through the cosmos and the sea, across the varied spaces of the world, and into the quiet corners of the soul. Some pieces wrestle with existentialism, others with the turbulence of human relationships, while some stand as fierce declarations of identity and defiance.

Together, they weave a narrative of transformation, loss, resilience, and hope.

The voices within these pages belong to time travellers and storm-watchers, butterfly collectors and unchained spirits.

They speak of stars that burn, of birds who cage themselves, of ships that refuse to sink, of daughters who carve their own paths, and of orphans of yesterday and globetrotters of today.

They are reflections of all that is ephemeral yet eternal, fragile yet unyielding.

Some of these words will resonate with you. Others may unsettle you.
But every verse invites you to feel—deeply, fully, unapologetically.
Let the words drift into you. Let them settle. Let them stir.

This book is not just a collection of poems. It is a dialogue between the past and the present, between chaos and peace, between the world and the self.

Read, reflect, and—most of all—feel.

Acknowledgements

To my mother, whose vision shapes the way I perceive the world - You are the quiet muse behind every thought, the unspoken lyric interspersed between the lines. Every word I smith, carries the beat of your heart and every emotion I experience, is the quintessence of your spirit.

To Memory, The timeless archivist of feeling - You have and continue to, file my lived experiences in words & images, filling the shelves of my heart. You bold sceptic, always questioning the linearity of time, teaching me that the past is not a place lost to time, but a liminal space between wakefulness and dreaming.

To People, motifs in the intricate embroidery of my mind, some sewn in gold, others in grey - You appear here not as you were, but as you were felt, transformed by my imagination, woven on the loom of memory and dyed by time. Whether you passed through my life like seasons or stayed rooted beside me like old-growth trees, you continue to embellish the fabric of these poems, softly and indelibly.

To Time, The inevitable and omnipotent force, both creator and eraser, keeper of memory and thief of people - Within your passage, I have lost and I have found. I have learned to forget and to remember and in oscillating between remembrance and forgetting, between loss and serendipity, I have learned to feel.

Without you, this book would not have been possible. These verses are not merely recollection, imagination, or expression.
They sway between what was and what might have been, what is and what could be.

They are shaped by all of you.

Contents

1. My Mother, The Sunflower

There was once a sunflower,
Tall, strong, and bright.
Her cheery face reflected
The colours of daylight.

She had a celestial child,
A daughter we know as the Sun.
From east to west each day,
This fiery child would run.

The sunflower, with love,
Upon her mighty child gazed.
Wherever The Sun moved,
Towards her, The Sunflower faced.

As dusk turned into night,
"Goodnight, Mum," The Sun said.
Saddened, the old sunflower
Lowered her doddering head.

Over the field, the next day,
Again, The Sun began to soar.
The sunflower raised her head,
For she was unhappy no more.

But then, one night,
The sunflower withered away.
On the brown, moist soil,
Her wilted petals lay.

At the break of dawn,
Up the Sun came.
Her rays scanned the field,
But it didn't look the same.

Now, at every sunrise,
Winces the Sun in pain
"My sunflower is gone,
Alas! I rose again."

2. Her Daughter, The Sun

At daybreak, she rose in a pink-gold flame,
But the field below her didn't look the same.
For her sunflower, she searched with a desperate gaze,
Through morning mist and evening haze.

Where once had swayed that cheery face,
Now lay an empty, barren space.
No stem stood tall to track her flight,
No petals turned up to drink her light.

So the sun raged in seething might;
A grieving daughter, fire and light.
Said the sun, "This can't be right;
Of my sunflower, I cannot lose sight."

Hence, down she fell through the endless space,
To reach her sunflower's resting place.
The sky behind her, blinded by light,
As she plunged forward with absent fright.

At last, she reached the arid field,
Where a sorrowed scene itself revealed.
Wilted petals she kissed, then lay
Beside her sunflower's unmarked grave.

The wind wailed to the morose moonlight,
"Watch! The sun grieves in her mother's rite.
Still conflagrant, still fierce and grand,
Lighting up the earth with her many radiant hands.

Though within her core, a dark shadow grows,
She remains ablaze amid her throes.
And she mourns, even though she stands tall;
The mighty sun, yes, but a daughter above all!"

3. Destiny's Father

It was a sunny winter noon
At the park were father and she
When a Sycamore caught her eye
And towards it she pranced in glee.

"Oh Dear Father!"
exclaimed Destiny,
"No matter how high,
I'll climb this tree.
I know I can scale it
even though it's really tall,
Will you have my back
if I slip or fall?"
Destiny's father looked up at her,
But before he could reply, some men he heard:

"Is she your daughter?" asked one,
"She speaks her mind with reckless abandon.
She is a woman now, but she's still the same;
Someday she'll bring you naught but shame."

Angrily said a second voice
"She is an aberration,
Refuses to abide by
accepted social conventions.

She needs to be put in place –
her little bubble burst.
She won't lower her voice,
And she puts herself first."

A third man complained,
"Look at her, unabashed, vain,
Ambitious, unrestrained,
going against the grain.

Impervious to our advances,
claims she's not here to please;
She says she'll live as she wants
until her breaths cease."

Groaned, the fourth man,
"She said she won't be a wife or mother.
If that's the kind I seek, then
I should look for another.

I told her: 'It's a man's world,
and she must learn
That her vehement aplomb
will be crushed at every turn.

Her ways are wayward –
to them she shouldn't stick.
Obedient wife, sacrificial mother
are the boxes a woman must tick.'"

The first man again, "Is she your daughter?
Is she even a girl?
If she is, clip her wings
before they further unfurl.

In this world of 'his',
there are rules for 'her' –
Prevalent through the ages,
that cannot be blurred."

Father, in deep thought
had been silent all along,
Listening to these men saying
that his daughter was wrong.

Far into the distance,
he looked for a while,
Then he turned towards them
with a seraphic smile.

His gentle voice,
the silence broke,
then the mild-mannered man
finally spoke.

"Yes, she is my daughter –
yes, she is a girl,
But she will not be subdued
by anyone in this world.

You say she's loud –
you call her vain,
It's because she won't wear
your archaic chain.

You think she is an aberration
for she speaks her mind,
Dares to bend the rules
that men like you designed.

You want her grovelling –
submissive and afraid,
To weep in the shadows,
to fade in the shade.

No. She will loom large;
Loud will she roar,
And I will encourage her
to always aim for more.

Yes, she is my daughter –
'Destiny' is her name,
A storm that no man
will silence or tame.

She calls me 'Father,'
and with pride I stand,
Beside my child,
her hand in my hand.

She wasn't put on Earth
to shrink herself for others,
to be a subservient wife
or a sacrificial mother.

A flock? If that's her choice –
or perhaps she'll roam,
Explore faraway lands,
and call the world her home.

I've taught her well
that love isn't servitude;
She's been raised to be kind,
yet strong and shrewd.

Your conventional boxes are
too small for her to fit –
Your minds too unevolved
to fathom her strength and grit.

I didn't bring her up
to pander to anyone –
She has been built up,
to be her own person.

You say, 'Clip her wings,
before they spread wide;'
Try it, and you'll find me
fighting by her side.

I know one day
my time will come to an end,
And I won't be here
to guide her or to defend.

But I will have raised her
so fierce, tough, and wise,
That she won't need me
after time has closed my eyes.

She will stand strong alone;
she will walk tall,
She'll live the life she wants –
she will have it all.

Yes, she is my daughter –
yes, she is a girl,
And she will live like a man
in a man's world.

4. Supernova

A star has fallen tonight,
Behold its dying light.
Through the stellar realm, watch it fall,
And in darkness, leave us all.

For you and I are cosmic dust,
Leftovers of the stars that birthed us.
We too shall disappear without a trace,
Into an icy, dreary, fathomless space.

Event horizon, here, no embers stay,
Only solemn silence slithers in slow decay.
All lights wane, all forms cease,
Sucked swiftly into an infinite abyss.

The universe will not recall
Or mourn us, stars that split and fall.
There's no heaven, no hell, there is just a void.
When we die, we're nothing; we're destroyed.

5. Two Orphans

"Oh, Yesterday's child,
You've lost your way.
There was no one to guide you,
So you strayed.
There is no one to stop me,
So I roam.
If there were such a place,
I'd have taken you home."

"Oh, today's youth,
Your eyes still gleam
With tears left behind
From our mother's unfulfilled dream.
I followed the known road,
Yet it led me astray.
Now home is a memory
That has faded away."

6. Lest they are forgotten

She sings the songs of her forgotten heroes,
Lest they remain unsung,
Carrying them in her heart,
Lest they come undone.

Her people before her,
Her heroes of old
Their stories she will tell,
Lest they remain untold.

Through dark, distressed nights,
On a sleepless streak,
Listening to their voice notes,
For the dead can no longer speak.

Remembering the hurt,
So she won't cease to feel,
Picking at her wounds,
Lest they start to heal.

Through her mind's meandering maze,
Half-forgotten songs,
Flipping through old photographs,
Lest she forget where she belongs.

She is their flesh and blood,
She has inherited their name.
What was stolen from them,
She is back to claim.

Their fight is now hers,
So is their pain.
The phoenix from the ashes
Behold! She rises again.

7. Endeavour and Destiny

Their world fell silent, freshly torn.
The siblings now orphaned, alone.
No mother's cuddles, no father's embrace,
Just lost voices echoing in a sepia space.

Their opulent house now felt unkind,
Each room a ghost, each wall a bind.
What once was home now felt so strange,
So they sought new skies, sought a change.

Endeavour said, "Sister, we must roam,
And turn the world into our makeshift home."
Said Destiny, "Brother, I think you're right.
Our heart's unlit; let's go somewhere bright."

So Endeavour and Destiny, soul and spark,
Set forth together from their homeland's ark.
Stardust they were, their spirits defined,
The pulse of their world, its rhythm aligned.

At first, through Central Asia they rode,
Across the steppes, as eagles soared.
The wind whispered of warriors and wheat,
As they plodded through snow with blistered feet.

Curious wanderers, side by side,
Endeavour and Destiny, with maps and guides.
Two souls bound not by fate alone,
But by a childhood shared, a bond strong grown.

They wandered through Thailand's luminous nights,
From temples bathed in numinous light,
To limestone caves that chanted of old,
And beachside parties, bright and bold.

They weren't just escaping sorrow's blight,
But hoping to muster the courage to fight.
He pulled back his grief like an ebbing tide;
Her throbbing ache she couldn't hide.

High up, they climbed through Nepal's sparse air,
Dragging the weight of their colossal gear.
From Himalayan loops, where prayer flags flew,
They watched the soul of the mountain renew.

Endeavour—quiet, the younger one,
With untold tales of inner battles won.
Destiny, the older, passionate and free,
Met every storm with fierce tenacity.

They sought peace in Kyoto's temple bells,
Smiling at trees as cherry blossoms fell.
In bazaars of Istanbul, by citadels and mosques,
They tasted spices, took souvenirs from treasures lost.

Sauntering through Marrakech's story and song,
And souks and taverns where caravans thronged,
They sipped mint tea in the heart of Fez,
And smelt frankincense on the old town's breath.

Each place they visited, each trail they took,
They chronicled it in their mother's book.
No more the want for maps to see—
They were each other's true country.

Through memories and photos, old jokes and songs,
They held on to where they truly belonged.
For love like theirs, familial and true,
Needs no instruction manual to follow through.

A roaming life soon let them see:
From pain and sorrow none are free.
Loss can claim everything we love,
But we must strive to rise above.

Though love for their lost would always remain,
By now they had learnt to find joy again.
In Mombasa's drums and coastal fire,
Their laughter rose; to live, they aspired.

In Rio's streets, they spun and swayed,
Dancing to samba beats in a Mardi Gras parade.
When Atacama's quiet amplified their sighs,
They whistled to the wind beneath red-hued skies.

In the Maldives' islands, with their sparkling lagoons,
Where sharks shimmered beneath a silver moon—
Amidst blue atolls, staring at the horizon's gleam,
They spoke of dreams they hadn't yet dreamed.

Sailing through fjords in the northern seas,
They saw glaciers weep into sliding scree.
In the Finnish Lapland, chasing northern lights,
They watched as foxes flit from sight.

From gondolas through Venice's liquid lanes,
They gazed at the moonlit windowpanes.
In Cairo, where saffron Sahara greets,
They explored pyramids in the sweltering heat.

From unknown ports to secluded peaks,
They learnt that silence sometimes speaks.
And in the world's vast, ever-changing face,
Their bond remained steadfast in each place.

And though the world was strange and wide,
They knew no journey was too great to stride.
As long as they wandered, hand in hand,
Two halves of a compass, exploring the land.

And whenever the road would rise or bend,
Each other's broken hearts they would mend.
For no matter where their feet would roam,
When together, they were always home.

8. An Urn of Souls

Its ancient hieroglyph, undeciphered,
Unnoticed beneath scarlet tides.
In the dark, dank depths of time,
An urn of souls hides.

Clusters of ruined buildings and dying towns,
Trapped in the debris of brick and sand.
Mortal rifts across the earth
Mar the face of the promised land.

My soul, in this urn of souls,
Will be in here until it is not.
These cold ceramic walls have sheltered
Failing minds and gasping thoughts.

Oh, kindred soul from my urn,
This claustrophobia you must fear not,
For beyond these wounded walls of old,
The places are with terror fraught.

There is a silence within these walls,
Sacred, untarnished, masking the roar
The roar of this bruised city,
A city with cacophonous chaos at its core.

9. Unvanquished

I fear no gale, no turbulent tide.
For I'm my daughter's courage, I'm my mother's pride.

I'm one's rudder and another's sail.
I will not falter, I will never fail.

I'm the hull that has stayed afloat, through tumultuous
tempests past.
I steer unyielding; strong, swift, steadfast.

Mist may rise, squalls may wail,
I'll reach ashore through scorch and hail.

Charting my course through waters wide,
I am my compass, I'm my guide.

I'm the anchor and I'm the mast;
Unvanquished, unbroken, I'm built to last.

10. The Last Inn before The Dark

An unfettered child careened down a road, linear,
Basking in the sunshine, with her mother near.
Gazing at finches prattling in the trees,
And at fresh spring leaves, pirouetting in the balmy breeze.
This scenic road was the one road I knew,
Knew no other; do children ever do?

Then one morning I woke, and I was all grown up,
I set forth from home to fill my life's curious cup.
Two seemingly endless roads before me lay,
A signpost read: *If you choose a road, on it you'll stay.*

The road to the right was the widely accepted one,
Paved, well-trodden, lit well by the sun.
Lines drawn clearly, with rules and maps,
And cautionary tales filled in, to even out its gaps.

Generations had walked it, heads held high,
With voices of those before them guiding nearby.
It was honoured, respected, a road well known,
With societal endorsement etched into every stone.

But to walk that path, a compromise was clear:
To mould myself for others, year after year,
To sacrifice my autonomy for the world's praise,
To wear a soft mask until the end of my days.

To be submissive, To take less space,
To make myself small, With a smile on my face.
To be nice, To be liked, To be confined
To live a life shaped by hands that weren't mine.

The other road was a road hardly defined.
It was enshrouded in fog and by a few ever lined.
No cogent reason given, they just called it wrong,
With no words of advice to guide one along.

With judgement galore and a dissident's strife,
But a possibility for one to command their own life.
The freedom to choose their own losses and gains,
To be the only bringer of their own joys and pain.

I stood at the crossroad, with a pivotal decision to make
To culminate in conformity or rebel for self's sake.
So I chose the path that very few knew,
To wade through the fog and carve my own way
through.

Seasons kept rolling till one day my steps grew slow,
And both roads met where old spirits go
The last inn before dark, the one with an
inextinguishable light,
Where tired travellers gather before fading into the
night.

There I saw the souls from the well-trodden way,
Their faces wearing a weariness, their spirits spirited
away.
Their experiences were similar, their tales humdrum,
Of forfeiture of their desires to appease, to conform.

Their voices lacked the spark that sets the spirit aflame,
Their narratives too uniform, their hearts just the same.
Then I turned to those who had trod my rugged path,
Their eyes whimsical, smiles warmer than the inn's
hearth.

Their stories original, their experiences profound,
Steeped in flamboyant flavours, of a life lived unbound.
Their hearts at peace, no envy in their voice,
For the lives they lived, were the lives of their choice.

And when the time came for us to bid our spirits loose,
I felt happy for, the unknown path I did choose.
For life isn't meant merely to fit, into the mould others
design,
But to be lived on your own terms, for your own self to
find.

11. The Time Traveller

Through epochs lost and histories made,
Since Earth breathed in a primordial shade,

I saw lands divide and shift,
Felt continents in silent drift.

I hunted beasts with sharpened bone,
Carved runes in caves, unseen, unknown.

I lit fires in the age of ice,
Then witnessed new civilisations rise.

I raised obelisks in Egypt's sand,
Built pyramids high with calloused hands.

I stacked the slabs of a pharaoh's throne,
But bore no credit on his haughty tombstone.

I marched through Troy as the towers fell,
Heard Cassandra's warning swell.

I saw the Senate's daggers gleam,
As Caesar collapsed with his ambitious dream.

I saw Rome rise in golden might,
Then Constantinople crumble in the night.

I saw a sultan rise and reign,
To assert the Ottomans' daring domain,

Then disperse like mist in fleeting breath
One kingdom's birth, another's death.

I saw Genghis paint the land
With fire and blood at his command.

I stood in Florence, art brush in hand,
As Renaissance reason reshaped the land.

The Bastille was stormed with rage untamed,
Yet the guillotines remained.

I saw shackles shattered in vain,
As masters forged new fetters again.

I saw lofty ships set sail with pride,
Heard clanking chains—those to the decks they tied.

I walked through fields of cotton white,
Where women and children wept at night.

I saw their backs lashed raw with hate,
Whipped, bought, sold—down on their fate.

I walked through lands where skin colour defined
The worth of souls, their rights assigned.

I saw apartheid's repugnant rule,
Systems built on lines so cruel.

I heard people pray, I heard them sing
Songs of freedom with broken wings.

I cowered in trenches with the stench of death,
As fields turned red by the men who power covet.

I stood in rooms where treaties were signed,
Where illusions of peace were tactically designed.

I rode through smoke in factory towns,
Where children toiled, their innocence drowned.

I wore the banners, marched in lines,
Then saw solidarity subside in time.

I witnessed women take their place
On fields, in factories, in offices, in space.

They fought, they laboured, they flew, they learned,
Yet true respect was never earned.

They worked the hours, dealt with feuds,
Still at home, were expected to be in servitude.

For still the world, though changing fast,
Takes from us first, gives to us last.

Though smaller built, we're asked for more
To match, to surpass, and still be ignored.

For no matter where, no matter when,
The world has been ruled by ruthless men.

Through bloodshed, ruin, false hopes, and fear,
Their reign prevailed for thousands of years.

I've lived through a million years and more,
Yet walked the same familiar shore.

For every age, in every land,
My kind's fate was drawn by another's hand.

A peasant's wife or a king's bride
A vassal, in thrall, until she died.

A girl, embarrassed by an older man's stare,
A woman the target of lust and despair.

For every throne that was won,
Women were sullied, their dignity undone.

For every war a powerful man raised,
Ordinary women, with their bodies, paid.

Now, I turn to future skies,
To years where no one has yet arrived.

I travel beyond the world we know,
To see if time has let us grow.

Perhaps ahead, beyond this tide,
The world has stepped over into a brighter side.

Or will I find, even in a new century's glow,
That all has changed, yet all is so?

12. The Seaward End

The sea, she lies in a restful repose,
A briny breath the current bestows.
White waves yaw over the reef,
Teasing a boat, just like the wind a dead leaf.

A tired tide moves calm and slow,
Over ochre sands in ebb and flow.
Seagulls soar through the salted sky,
Wispy white ribbons wheeling high.

Beyond cliffs of green where waters gleam,
Where kelp sways slow in turquoise streams.
Schools of herrings race in delirious delight,
Like shooting stars on a warm summer night.

In her watery arms, the moonbeam sways,
Soft silver trails on undulating waves.
With a cradle vast, this mother mild,
The sea sings to the moonlight, her sleeping child.

Fishermen at dawn's first light
Cast their nets on waters bright.
A marine harvest's motherly embrace,
The sea provides with resolute grace.

The sea, with her magnanimous hands,
Feeds many mouths in distant lands.
Large hulls traverse from shore to shore,
As liquid roads the world explores.

But beneath that shimmering endless blue
Lies a void no light imbues.
Ships like giants lick its crest,
Yet sink as phantoms laid to rest.

Famed voyagers and armadas that sail
Turn into spectral wrecks, their names curtailed.
She bore the keels of Rome and Crete,
Then swallowed empires and their mighty fleets.

The seabed keeps what men let slip
Treasures and wreckage, mast and ship.
She murmurs of the ones she keeps,
Those who sank to the fathomless deep.

Their bones now pearls, their ribs now caves,
Their dreams now swallowed by the waves.
And oh, how ruthless, cold, and grim,
A tempest wakes at her whim.

Like Charybdis with her mouth agape,
She grants no mercy, no escape.
And still, I stand at her heaving breast,
In love, in awe, in quiet unrest.

Each step I take, she pulls me near,
Her whispers low, yet sharp and clear.
The sea, the sea, she sings to me,
In wet blue murmurs, unhinged and free.

She shrieks, she wails, she laughs, she hums,
A restless force, a war-drum's thrum.
Her waves, they dance in ecstatic glee,
They curl like fingers and beckon me.

Sunlight shatters on her tepid skin,
In a siren's lure, in Poseidon's grin.
She calls me down, she calls me deep,
Beyond the realm of wake or sleep.

She croons, she pleads, she sings, she sighs,
She grasps me tight with her deep blue eyes.
The tide ascends, the air turns thin,
Salt fills my lungs; she pulls me in.

And though I know what lies below,
I do not fight, I do not slow.
For the sea's summon, I must obey
Into her depths, I must drift away.

No fear, no fight, no regret, no sound,
Just the sea dark, and her love unbound.

13. The Man called 'The Rose'

He lived a life of obscurity,
In the quietest part of a noisy city.
A sombre smile upon his face,
He walked alone with a gentle pace.

An child born of horror and fear,
No mother's love in his tender years.
He grew in shadows, cold and dim,
Yet kindness blossomed inside of him.

He toiled for those who'd never stay,
Gave his all, still, they walked away.
He longed to matter, to belong,
But lived unheard, an unsung song.

He longed for arms to draw him near,
For loving words, for voices dear.
In a selfish world, through time unkind,
Perhaps love wasn't his to find.

Now heaven has claimed his sorrowed soul
No voices mourn, no church bells toll.
No tearful prayers, no eyes red,
It's just another day, though *The Rose* is dead.

Too late, too late, he died alone,
He died unloved, he died unknown.
Too late, too late, he died unseen,
Dreaming of how his life could have been.

At his grave, I stand with love untold
Too late to tell, too late to hold.
He longed to be loved, he longed to be,
Yet never knew how much he mattered to me.

"Oh, lost Rose of Summer,
Your remains though in this cold place lay.
In the warm confines of her heart,
You'll always stay

Unhurt by death,
Untouched by decay."

14. Distorted Frequencies

Bright and swift, like a comet ablaze,
Then plummets into herself, weathered and dazed.

Her words fail as her thoughts race
In a water stain on the subway wall, she sees her face.

Memories burn inside her head,
Like Roman candles, fiery red.

Shop signs and neon lights, in patterns bizarre,
In puddles on the road, at the midnight hour.

Incessant whispers, in meaningless noise,
Aurora borealis, in her eyes.

Sparks fly from the tracks, screeching goes the train.
The empty platform glistens, in the concave of a drop of
rain.

15. Bipolarity

I cauterise, burn, seal its frayed edges,
Yet they leak in varying stages
The sanguinary streams
From the sarcophagus of my heart.

I think I'll smother me not, but this thought is insane!
Put a silver lining to the pain?
Warp the laws of time and space,
And let the bull's-eye hit the unreleased dart?

But then I hear my screams, through a vertigo,
Hear a blaring echo fading slow,
And with my fingertips, pull the fragments of
This fractured mind apart.

No, I'll just paint over this caustic stain,
Douse it in gasoline, envelope it in flames,
Hold the pendulum, reverse the hands,
And once again, I'm going back to the start.

16. Wings and Wear

He was as free as the wind
Under the boundless sky,
A bird with mighty wings
Who no longer wanted to fly.

He had built himself a cage,
A gilded one,
Fitted it with a strong door,
Which he had left open.

For maybe someday
He'd want to fly,
Like other birds
In the bright blue sky.

That day didn't come,
And time rolled on.
He lived happily,
Sang his mirthful song.

Then one day, he said,
"The skies now I seek."
He fluttered his wings,
But they had grown weak.

At the door of his cage,
In anguish, he stood
"I wish I flew
When I still could."

17. Once

Scatter the pieces of your heart,
Scatter them with a careless hand;
Watch them sail on sun-kissed waves
To the endless horizon's unmapped end.

Hear! The nightingale sings a song,
Hear, for she may not sing again;
Let the melody waft through
Your lonely mind and its dusty lanes.

Watch the moon hanging high,
A silver bauble in a diamond sky;
It has lived longer than you and I,
Yet it whispers that the end is nigh.

From earth to sky stretches a bridge
This journey you have to take:
Eons long, needle narrow,
Yet haste you have to make.

Oh, my love, just live for once,
For you may never live again;
Let life not be a memory
Of a million breaths drawn in vain.

18. August Blossoms

August showers, and it has sprung up again.
The little lantana, fragile yet vain,
With its yellow blossoms, bold and bright,
Flailing its flimsy boughs in the high-noon light.

It bloomed last season, and the one before
An unbidden guest I choose to ignore.
I won't water it, yet it'll grow;
It'll soak up the rain, breathe in the sun's soft glow.

In the morning breeze, it'll dance carefree,
Tattle on me to the old oak tree.
It'll tease me that it doesn't need me
I'll pay it no heed; it's so ordinary.

Soon its leaves will fall off, one by one,
Carried by the wind, their journeys done.
To grassy graves, both near and far,
I'll feel no loss, nor bear a scar.

I never planted it, nor cared to try
It's an unwanted weed; why would I?
In this world so many die;
No one cares, so why should I?

Yet, some October morning soon,
Beneath a weary, sinking moon,
With the sun bleeding red in the sky,
I'll see the bare twigs, and I will sigh.

My heart will ache, though it wasn't my own,
But in my garden, for a time it had grown.
Though I never wanted it, I'll still cry,
Though I'll always know that it'll again come by.

Love grows quietly as time slips by,
And who can be sure of a chance at goodbye?
So I'll mourn today for what's to come,
Before its arrival leaves me numb.

My yellow lantana, soon you'll go
I don't love you, that I know.
Never planted you, but still I'll mourn,
For your absence will weigh more than my scorn.

Today, near your vibrant blooms,
I cradle loss before the doom.
Grieving now, in desolate dismay,
And some tears, I fear, may slip away.

So let me weep until the sadness dries,
Before the final, farewell sigh.
For pain foreseen, though yet to come,
Feels like a wound already done.

19. Lights in the Night

I was out tending my garden,
When an elderly lady came to me
She said she was my neighbour
though her, I may have never seen.

I smiled at her and said
that I've seen her many a time,
that the lines on her face remind me
of my mother's forehead lines.

With a gentle touch, she held my hand
and asked if I were alright ,
for she'd seen all my lights on
at one and two and three in the night.

I assured her I was fine,
but someone else might not be.
I keep my lights switched on
so in the darkness, some light they'll see.

In the house across from mine
lives a nurse with her children three.
She is out working all night,
so my lights are on for her girls to see.

So if someday, at a late hour,
for a mother, there a need be,
they'll see these guiding lights
and for help reach out to me.

And in the house next door to them
lives a man whose folks are forever gone.
He paces across his roof
from midnight until dawn.

When his gaze travels here,
My glowing lights his eyes see,
and in those lonely hours,
they keep him company.

And sometimes, I see a lady
returning home late.
She slows down near my house,
takes a brief stop at my gate.

For a woman the night can be frightening,
so while walking, quick steps she takes.
When she sees my lights, she knows
the lady who lives here is still awake.

She sees this place as safe,
so to catch her breath, this pause she takes,
and she gulps down some water
before the rest of her journey she makes.

So if you find yourself alone
in the dark of the night,
know that somewhere, someone's window
still glows with a kind, warm light.

Then, to the elderly woman I said,
"If you've been seeing my lights all night,
it must mean you've been staying awake
until the morning light.

And if you ever feel lonely,
or simply need company,
Please come over—you'll find me here,
with a warm kettle of tea."

20. A Restoration

She was a house with no windows,
And just one, but boarded door.
Inside were elegant rooms
Where exquisite artwork she stored.

This house once had an occupant
Who had vandalised her walls;
So she nailed that one door shut
To restrict access to her halls.

Across the street stood an artist,
Who had no place to call home.
He wished for a lasting roof over his head,
For he wasn't of those who roam.

His last house had innumerable windows,
They let in too much light;
It didn't feel like home to him,
As it was noisy and too bright.

He dreamt of a windowless house
To take shelter inside,
A quiet shade to call home,
Where he wouldn't have sleepless nights.

When he came across this house,
He knew this place was the one.
For months, at the door he called,
But the locks wouldn't come undone.

Then one day he picked up a paintbrush
And started beautifying the boarded door.
Then, just like that, one nail came off,
And in the next few months, a few more.

By now he had painted the door,
And refurbished the cladding tiles;
The house exterior looked prettier
Than it had in many a while.

He picked up the fallen nails
And left to cast them far away;
Upon his return, he saw
On the porch steps a few more lay.

Smiling, he climbed up the roof,
Replaced the shingles that had worn out.
When he came back down to the portico,
He saw the boards scattered about.

He knew the house had no windows
But what if she needed a little light?
So he went to the store and bought a lamp
That could illuminate her at night.

Then outside he built a jasmine garden,
Embellished it with vibrant gnomes;
When he walked up to the door that day,
There lay a doormat that read, "Welcome Home."

21. Summer Storms and Twilight Trails

I stand on my balcony,
Sipping my coffee, bitter and dark.
Soft sunrays caress my face,
And I hear the quavering of a distant lark.

Beyond the treeline, beyond the trails,
A storm is brewing, heavy and slow.
The wind whirls in the sweltering heat,
And in the air, dust particles glow.

Black nimbus clouds, like ink on wet paper,
Spread slowly across the grey-blue sky.
Tree nests worry that waylaid birds
May get pulled into the storm's eye.

I watch the wind unspool the threads
That held together the fabric of this day.
I hear the howl of inclement weather
As branches bend, then break away.

A cloudburst pounds the forest mercilessly,
And in this ruin, I find release.
If it is already gone, there is no fear of losing,
So chaos is the perfect peace.

When all is calm, my mind still whispers,
"This won't last, it never does."
Peace portends its own ending
So peaceful times, I dare not trust.

Summer storms are chaos disguised
They rage, they uproot, pull everything apart.
The strong they bear, the weak they tear,
Then leave behind a brand-new start.

Tomorrow, when the storm has passed,
I'll walk the forest trails at twilight.
Where there were trees, there'll be trails anew,
While overtrodden paths will have been shrouded from
sight.

For now, I stand and sip and ponder
The storm in me, the storm outside.
Tomorrow's twilight trails will answer
If I hide in chaos, or if in me it hides.

22. The Tempest Friend

You don't know me, but I know you,
You're broken but still pulling through,
Repeating past mistakes, breaking further,
Then putting back the shards together.

I won't let you find me today.

When you're done with your lows and highs,
When your soul is tired but wise,
Towards the end when you're worn,
When you're frail and can't go on.

It's then when I'll come to you.

Not as a lover, not as a foe,
But as a shadow in a bright, white glow.
Not with a whisper, nor with a cry,
But as a ceased breath, as the last sigh.

No regret, no pain, no past to bear,
Just silence and an unblinking stare.
So do as you will until your time is through,
I'll then come and I'll take you.

23. Immutable, I

Every season you find yourself in,
You'll find a different me.

The child, the youth, the elder
Are illusions that you see.

The child learned, the youth sought,
What time wrought, the elder taught.

Now I'm here, soon I'll be gone.
In an ephemeral body I was born,

But I'm no face, no definite form,
No tangible limit, no physical norm.

I can take you where your feet won't,
Hold you when your arms don't.

I'm within you and without,
Close as a shadow, without a doubt.

I'm the thoughts that you think
And the words that you write.

I'm your soul,
Immutable, infinite.

24. Little Ember

Little ember, bright alight,
In the darkest hour of the night,
No shadow of fright, no draught's might
Can ever smother your undying light.

Little ember, frail yet proud,
Darkness will never be your shroud.
You dwindle, you flicker, but still you fight,
In your silent mutiny against the sweeping night.

Little ember, small yet strong,
Through an endless night you burn along.
No open window, no tornado's din
Can steal the fire you hold within.

25. The Man at Sarracenia Square

I met a man at Sarracenia Square,
His form was poised, his manner fair.
His words were wise, rich with grace,
A kind smile adorned his beautiful face.

We spoke of art, of books and thought,
Of those we had lost and the battles we'd fought,
Of fleeting happiness in moments rare.
We laughed together and sorrows shared.

He said he was fond of nature's gleam,
Loved pretty things that stirred his heart to dream,
That beauty in nature held him in awe
Flowers and mountains, everything he saw.

Then, with a soft chuckle, he spoke of his prize
Beautiful butterflies he claims from the skies.
These dainty creatures, with vivid hues,
He keeps in jars, in a room painted blue.

He keeps them safe; he feeds them well,
Admires them from outside their crystal cell.
In delight, he watches them flutter their wings,
Thanks them for the joy they bring.

He loves them, so with them he never parts,
Even when time stops their fragile hearts.
He then gently pins them, to a board ,
Their bodies dead, as though alive, posed.

He took my hand, said how beautiful I was,
Declared his love, smiled, then took a pause
I thanked him politely, I could tell his love was true,
But his kind of love, I could not approve.

A butterfly collector I met at Sarracenia Square
He loved me I know, but I left him there.
For love should serve as your wings when you fly,
Not capture and hold, then watch you die.

26. Destiny and The Butterfly Collector

Destiny:

"Oh Butterfly Collector from Sarracenia Square,

Your manners are gentle, your gravitas rare.

You're kind, and with morals well-defined,

Your wisdom and knowledge speak to my curious mind.

With a pleasant face; a sight for sore eyes

You spill your heart without a hint of lies.

You speak of love with a gaze sincere,

But something about you instils in me fear".

The Butterfly Collector:

"I lost my heart at Sarracenia Square,

To your twinkling eyes and jet-black hair.

To your laughter loud, the passion of a flame

I was left spellbound when you uttered my name.

A vibrant future with you I seek,

For you can fill colours in my world bleak.

What I offered you was my tender care

But alas, you mistook it for a snare".

Destiny:

"You spoke of wings stolen from the skies,

Of beauty kept behind crystal lies.

For you, love is to hold, to bind and confine

But in a golden cage, love I don't want to find".

The Butterfly Collector:

"Where you see a cage, I see a shrine,

Where fragile wings could always safely shine.

The world is cruel, but I am strong

I only wish to keep you from all that can go wrong".

Destiny:

"I'm my father's daughter, Destiny is my name.

I won't be a mute spectator of my own life's game.

I won't be pinned to suit anyone's view,

For I must flutter my wings in my own skies of blue.

In a jar I can't live, for I'm born to soar

I've heard of captive love from people before.

They praised my vivacity, yet wanted to still my pace,

For me to warm their hearth, but to extinguish my own

blaze".

The Butterfly Collector:
"I never can imagine causing you pain;
I simply hoped with me, forever you'd remain.
Whenever I cherish someone, they just want to flee,
When all I wish is, for them to stay with me.".

Destiny:
"Your love is faithful, but you're not right for me;
The fear I feel, you aren't able to see.
You wish for a forever love and so do I
But you choose to confine; I choose to let fly.
How tragic it is that someone's affection
by stifling another, morphs into possession
I won't choose a sad life, I'll choose a sad goodbye
And I wish you good luck with your next butterfly".